GRANDMOTHER'S
GIFT *of*
MEMORIES

GRANDMOTHER'S GIFT of MEMORIES

AN AFRICAN–AMERICAN FAMILY KEEPSAKE

DANITA
ROUNTREE GREEN

Illustrations by
JAMES RANSOME

A MARLENE CONNOR/BLACKBERRY PRESS PRODUCTION

BROADWAY BOOKS New York

To Alma,
my mother and first love,
1934–1996
—D. R. G.

BROADWAY

GRANDMOTHER'S GIFT OF MEMORIES.
Text copyright © 1997 Danita Rountree Green.
Illustrations copyright © 1997 James Ransome.
All rights reserved. Printed in Singapore.
No part of this book may be reproduced or
transmitted in any form or by any means, elec-
tronic or mechanical, including photocopying,
recording, or by any information storage and
retrieval system, without written permission
from the publisher. For information address
Broadway Books, a division of Bantam
Doubleday Dell Publishing Group, Inc.,
1540 Broadway, New York, NY 10036.

Broadway Books titles may be purchased for
business or promotional use or for special sales.
For information, please write to: Special
Markets Department, Bantam Doubleday Dell
Publishing Group, Inc., 1540 Broadway, New
York, NY 10036.

BROADWAY BOOKS and its logo, a letter B
bisected on the diagonal, are trademarks of
Broadway Books, a division of Bantam
Doubleday Dell Publishing Group, Inc.

FIRST EDITION

Designed by R studio T, New York City

ISBN 0-553-06746-X

97 98 99 00 01 10 9 8 7 6 5 4 3 2 1

CONTENTS

My Dearest Black Pearl,

I am your
GRANDMOTHER.
This is a title of honor and respect.
I am proud to be yours: to love you,
to guide you, and to teach you.
Many of our mothers and grandmothers stitched
fabric from their family's lived-in clothing into
quilts, with each strip and square
recalling memories.
Today I am stitching your name
into our family quilt and passing down
to you my greatest gift:
my memories.

FOR

_____

WITH ALL MY LOVE,

FROM _____

DATE_____

chapter 1

OUR
FAMILY
HISTORY

A life stitched together one piece at a time

Making somethin' out of nothin'

A fabric of rhyme

Blending colors like rhythm and patterns like prose

The quilt comes together as our family grows.

You

---------------------------   ---------------------------

---------------------------   ---------------------------

Mother   *Father*

-------------------   -------------------   -------------------   -------------------

-------------------   -------------------   -------------------   -------------------

Grandmother   *Grandfather*   *Grandmother*   *Grandfather*

-------------------   -------------------   -------------------   -------------------

-------------------   -------------------   -------------------   -------------------

*Great
Grandfather*   *Great
Grandfather*   *Great
Grandfather*   *Great
Grandfather*

-------------------   -------------------   -------------------   -------------------

-------------------   -------------------   -------------------   -------------------

*Great
Grandmother*   *Great
Grandmother*   *Great
Grandmother*   *Great
Grandmother*

OUR FAMILY REUNIONS

A family is two or more people bonded together by love, trust, commitment, or blood lineage.

A reunion is a coming together.

When we come together, our stories are retold for a new generation and our love is rewarded once again.

PREDOMINANT FAMILY SURNAMES_____

_____

_____

FAMILY HISTORIANS _____

_____

_____

YOU HAVE RELATIVES IN THESE STATES _____

_____

_____

IN OUR FAMILY THE OLD HOMESTEAD IS _____

_____

OUR FAVORITE PLACE TO HAVE REUNIONS IS_____

_____

_____

WHEN WE COME TOGETHER AS A FAMILY, WE LIKE TO ____

_____

_____

_____

MY MOTHER AND FATHER

*On the day I was born, my parents started a journey
that has led to you.*

[p h o t o]

MY MOTHER'S NAME _____

WHEN I THINK OF HER, _____

_____

_____

_____

_____

IN THIS PICTURE, _____

_____

_____

_____

MY FATHER'S NAME _____

WHEN I THINK OF HIM, _____

_____

_____

_____

_____

_____

IN THIS PICTURE, _____

_____

_____

_____

[p h o t o]

OTHER PEOPLE WHO RAISED ME

It takes an entire village to raise a child.
These are the people who watched and helped me grow.

MY GODPARENTS _____

_____

_____

_____

_____

OUR NEIGHBORHOOD RELATIVES AND FRIENDS _____

_____

_____

_____

_____

_____

_____

PASTOR, TEACHERS, SCOUT LEADERS, COACHES _____

_____

_____

_____

_____

_____

_____

_____

ABOUT OUR RELATIVES

My Baby Sunshine, you have many "ancestors." These are your grandparents' grandparents and so on back through time.

THE OLDEST RELATIVES WE CAN TRACE ARE _____

_____

_____

_____

_____

HERE'S WHAT WE KNOW ABOUT THEM _____

_____

_____

_____

_____

TALENTS THAT RUN IN OUR FAMILY ARE_____

_____

_____

_____

_____

THE MOST "FAMOUS" MEMBER OF OUR FAMILY IS _____

_____

PHYSICAL TRAITS THAT RUN IN OUR FAMILY ARE_____

_____

_____

_____

AND THE WINNER IS...

BEST JOKE TELLER _____

_____

BEST DANCER_____

_____

BEST SINGER _____

_____

BEST TALKER_____

_____

PRANKSTER _____

_____

FAVORITE EATS AND TREATS, AND WHO COOKS THEM

_____

_____

_____

_____

MY PRAYER FOR OUR FAMILY _____

_____

_____

_____

_____

_____

_____

_____

chapter 2

MY CHILDHOOD MEMORIES

Dark fingers stitching below and above

Piecing together a lifetime of love.

Clean scraps and old tatters through ebony fingers

Find new life and laughter where baby's breath lingers.

We grow up so quickly, but memories hold fast.

Each day becomes history creating our past.

YOUR GRANDMA AS A BABY

Sweet Pea, long ago I was a little bitty baby just like you. And from Heaven, the ancestors whispered my name.

MY GIVEN NAME _____

WHO NAMED ME _____

THE NAME WAS CHOSEN BECAUSE _____

_____

MY NICKNAMES_____

_____

WHEN THIS PHOTO WAS TAKEN

I WAS____ YEARS OLD.

IN THIS PICTURE,_____

_____-

_____-

_____-

_____-

_____-

[photo]

[photo]

WHEN THIS PHOTO WAS TAKEN

I WAS____ YEARS OLD.

IN THIS PICTURE,_____

_____

_____

_____

_____

_____

I WAS BORN ON _____

AT _____

I WEIGHED_____AND WAS_____INCHES LONG

MY EYES WERE _____

MY HAIR WAS_____

MY MOST ENDEARING CHARACTERISTIC WAS_____

THE PEOPLE I RESEMBLED AS A BABY WERE _____

_____

AS I GOT OLDER, I STARTED TO LOOK MORE LIKE _____

_____

MY CHILDHOOD HOME

Toffee Treat, my home was full of character and voice, gesture and motion, that make me who I am today. Your home is a special place, too.

WHEN I WAS BORN, MY PARENTS WERE LIVING IN _____

_____

_____

THE BEST THINGS ABOUT THAT HOME WERE _____

_____

_____

_____

MY OWN "SPECIAL PLACE" WAS _____

_____

_____

MY CHORES INCLUDED _____

_____

_____

WHEN I WAS BORN, _____ WAS PRESIDENT.

WHAT A DOLLAR WOULD BUY _____

_____

_____

MY ALLOWANCE WAS _____

WHAT I BOUGHT WITH IT _____

_____

_____

_____

YOUR GRANDMA AS A LITTLE GIRL

MY VERY FIRST MEMORY IS _____

_____

_____

_____

I WORE MY HAIR _____

_____

MY FAVORITE OUTFITS WERE _____

_____

PETS WE HAD WERE _____

_____

FOR MY BIRTHDAYS, WE _____

_____

_____

I REMEMBER THINKING SOME THINGS WERE SPOOKY, LIKE _____

_____

_____

SOME OTHER THINGS MADE US LAUGH, LIKE _____

_____

_____

TO ME, A SPECIAL TREAT WAS _____

_____

MY FAVORITE TOY WAS _____

_____

WHAT I WANTED TO BE WHEN I GREW UP _____

_____

OUR CHURCH

One's legacy is akin to one's spirit, Sun Child.
Say Hallelujah and let your spirit dance.

WHEN I WAS A YOUNG GIRL, THE CHURCH WE ATTENDED WAS _____
_____
_____

DURING SUNDAY SCHOOL WE _____
_____
_____
_____
_____
_____
_____

SPECIAL CEREMONIES I REMEMBER BEING A PART OF WERE_____
_____
_____
_____
_____
_____
_____
_____
_____

OUR HOLIDAY TRADITIONS

These are those magic times of glitter and lights,
ribbon and laughter, prayer and remembrance.

EASTER _____
_____
_____

FOURTH OF JULY _____
_____
_____

THANKSGIVING _____
_____
_____

CHRISTMAS _____
_____
_____

NEW YEAR'S _____
_____
_____

MY FAVORITE HOLIDAY WAS _____

BECAUSE _____

SCHOOL DAYS

Grade school brings back memories of chalk dust, spelling bees, and times tables. I discovered my potential and learned how to dream.

WHEN I STARTED ATTENDING SCHOOL WE LIVED AT _____

_____

_____

_____

THE ELEMENTARY SCHOOL I ATTENDED WAS CALLED _____

_____

_____

PEOPLE TOLD ME THAT WHEN I FIRST WENT TO SCHOOL, I _____

_____

_____

MY FAVORITE TEACHERS WERE _____

_____

_____

MY GRADES WERE _____

_____

THE SUBJECTS I LIKED BEST WERE _____

_____

_____

AWARDS AND HONORS I WON INCLUDED _____

_____

_____

_____

AFTER SCHOOL, I WOULD _____

_____

_____

_____

_____

I GRADUATED IN _____

_____

_____

THE FRIENDS, NEIGHBORS, AND COUSINS I PLAYED WITH INCLUDED

_____

_____

_____

_____

_____

_____

IN THE SUMMERTIME, OUR FAMILY WOULD _____

_____

_____

_____

_____

_____

_____

MEMORIES OF GOOD FOOD

So many of my childhood memories center around food and family fun.
Whether at a dinner table or a picnic table,
some tastes and smells still remind me of home.

SOME OF THE EVERYDAY DINNERS I REMEMBER HAVING WERE _____

_____

_____

_____

_____

AND FOR DESSERT WE WOULD HAVE _____

_____

_____

_____

_____

MY FAVORITE PARTS AT A SUNDAY DINNER WERE _____

_____

_____

_____

_____

IT WAS A TREAT WHEN WE HAD _____

_____

_____

I WAS GOOD AT MAKING_____

_____

_____

RECIPES

chapter 3

MY TEENAGE MEMORIES

A piecing together, quick hands holding hearts,

Each square tells a story

Never ends once it starts.

Each piece very different but all part of the whole

The quilt comes together linking us soul to soul.

HIGH SCHOOL YEARS

Wonderful One, these were my years of discovery. They put the dip in my hips and the rhythm in my blues. Sometimes I was fearful but other times I was fearless. So hold on and enjoy the ride!

THE HIGH SCHOOL I ATTENDED WAS CALLED _____
_____
_____

WE WERE LIVING AT _____
_____
_____

IN HIGH SCHOOL, MY FAVORITE SUBJECT WAS _____
_____
_____

SOMETIMES I STAYED AFTER SCHOOL TO _____
_____
_____

BEING A TEENAGER MEANT THAT NOW I WANTED TO _____
_____
_____

OUR PROM WAS _____
_____
_____

HIGH SCHOOL GRADUATION WAS _____
_____
_____
_____

MY FRIENDS AND I HUNG OUT AT _____

_____

WE WENT TO DANCES AT_____

_____

AND PARTIES AT _____

_____

MY GOOD FRIENDS WERE _____

_____

_____

[photo]

IN THIS PICTURE,_____

_____

FEELING GROWN UP

My teenage years were like an intimate adventure, every twist and turn mapping out the young woman within.

MY SIMPLE WORLD BEGAN TO CHANGE WHEN _____

_____

_____

I REMEMBER FEELING INDEPENDENT WHEN I _____

_____

_____

I FELT SO PROUD WHEN_____

_____

_____

I WAS SO EMBARRASSED WHEN_____

_____

_____

WHAT I WANTED TO CHANGE ABOUT MY WORLD WAS _____

_____

_____

_____

I DIDN'T WANT ANYONE TO KNOW AT THE TIME, BUT I NOW CAN

SAY THAT I_____

_____

I'LL NEVER FORGET _____

_____

_____

I WORKED AS A _____

I EXPRESSED MY CREATIVITY BY _____

_____

I LEARNED TO DRIVE WHEN I WAS _____

THE CAR I LEARNED TO DRIVE ON WAS A _____

MY FAVORITE_____

    MOVIE STARS_____

    TV STARS_____

    PERFORMERS_____

    GROUPS_____

    SONGS _____

    CARS_____

WHO WAS CONSIDERED COOL AND WHAT WAS HOT_____

_____

_____

PEOPLE I ADMIRED _____

_____

WHAT I LIKED MOST ABOUT MYSELF_____

_____

_____

NOW WHEN I LOOK BACK ON MY HIGH SCHOOL YEARS, I REALIZE

HOW IMPORTANT THESE THINGS WERE_____

_____

TODAY I THINK THAT YOUNG PEOPLE SHOULD GET AN EDUCATION TO

_____

Precious One, these pages tell you a lot about me.
Come close—I am going to share some secrets with you.

MY FIRST CRUSH _____

_____

MY FIRST DATE _____

_____

_____

MY FIRST HEARTACHE _____

_____

_____

MY FIRST JOB_____

_____

MY FIRST TRAIN TRIP_____

MY FIRST PLANE TRIP_____

MY FIRST TRIP ON MY OWN_____

_____

MY FIRST BIG DECISION _____

_____

_____

MY FIRST REAL RESPONSIBILITY_____

_____

_____

_____

_____

STYLES HAVE CERTAINLY CHANGED

Cool, Groovy, Happening, Hot, Serious, Bad, Slammin'.
It's tough keeping up with the times!

WHEN I WAS A TEENAGER, GIRLS USED TO WEAR _____

_____

_____

AND THE GUYS WOULD WEAR _____

_____

_____

I REMEMBER ONE OF MY FAVORITE OUTFITS WAS _____

_____

HAIRSTYLES WERE_____

_____

OUR FAVORITE RADIO STATIONS WERE_____

_____

I GOT TO HEAR MUSIC PERFORMED LIVE WHEN _____

_____

_____

THE DANCES WE DID WERE _____

_____

SLANG THAT EVERYBODY WAS USING INCLUDED TERMS LIKE_____

_____

_____

_____

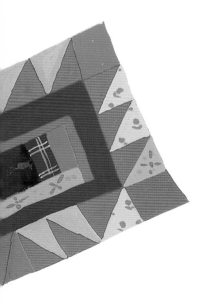

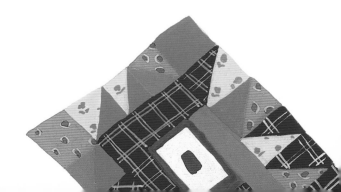

chapter 4

MY
GROWN-UP
MEMORIES

Our quilt stays together and weathers the years,

Ever present to warm me and harbor my tears.

It reflects all my joys and wishes, Sweet Pea.

A quilt is a comfort, like you are to me.

I WAS BECOMING A GROWN-UP

As you grow, you will be faced with decisions. Here are a few of mine, and the paths I chose to follow.

AFTER HIGH SCHOOL, THESE WERE PRIORITIES I SET FOR MYSELF_____

_____

_____

THOSE PRIORITIES BEGAN TO CHANGE WHEN_____

_____

_____

AFTER A WHILE, THERE WERE OTHER THINGS I WANTED TO ACCOMPLISH,

SUCH AS _____

_____

_____

MY BEST FRIENDS DURING THOSE YEARS WERE _____

_____

_____

FOR MOST OF MY LIFE I'VE BELIEVED IN THE IMPORTANCE OF _____

_____

_____

THOUGHTS AND THINGS THAT COMFORTED ME _____

_____

_____

MY WORK

*Every day we are making history. Right now, you are holding
my legacy in your hands.*

I CONTINUED MY EDUCATION AT _____

_____

_____

I BEGAN WORKING WHEN _____

_____

_____

MY FIRST BIG BREAK WAS _____

_____

_____

MY CAREER CHOICE WAS _____

_____

_____

OTHER THINGS I DECIDED I WANTED TO LEARN WERE _____

_____

_____

MY THOUGHTS ON GROWING UP AND LEAVING "THE NEST" _____

_____

_____

_____

WHERE MY HEART LED ME

I MET YOUR GRANDFATHER IN 19 _____ AT _____

_____

_____

_____

WHEN I GOT TO KNOW HIM A LITTLE BIT, I THOUGHT TO MYSELF,

_____

_____

_____

I LIKED HIM BECAUSE _____

_____

_____

_____

WHAT WE HAD IN COMMON WAS_____

_____

_____

_____

OUR COURTSHIP WAS _____

_____

_____

GUESS WHO PROPOSED TO WHOM! _____

_____

_____

_____

_____

YOUR GRANDFATHER

YOUR GRANDFATHER WAS BORN IN _____

_____ ON _____

HE WENT TO THESE SCHOOLS _____

_____

_____

HE HAS MADE HIS LIVING _____

_____

_____

HIS HOBBIES INCLUDE _____

_____

_____

HE LIKES TO SAY _____

_____

HIS BEST BUDDIES ARE _____

_____

_____

HIS FAVORITE MEAL IS _____

_____

YOU MAY NOT KNOW THIS ABOUT

YOUR GRANDFATHER _____

_____

_____

_____

IN THIS PICTURE, _____

_____

[photo]

OUR WEDDING

My search for love led me to your grandpa, and together we planned a life.
Our dreams always included a precious one like you.

WE WERE MARRIED ON _____

IN _____

THE PASTOR WAS _____

I WORE _____

AND YOUR GRANDFATHER WORE _____

THE WEDDING WAS _____

_____

SOME OF THE RELATIVES AND FRIENDS WHO ATTENDED WERE_____

_____

_____

[photo]

WHAT THE BRIDE WAS THINKING _____

OUR LIFE TOGETHER

THE FIRST PLACE WE LIVED TOGETHER WAS _____

_____

_____

SOME OF OUR MEMORABLE WEDDING GIFTS WERE _____

_____

_____

LATER WE MOVED TO _____

_____

MY IN-LAWS _____

EVENTS THAT CHANGED OUR LIVES IN THE EARLY YEARS WERE ____

_____

_____

_____

_____

WHEN TIMES GOT TOUGH I WOULD _____

_____

_____

_____

I STILL SMILE TO MYSELF WHEN I THINK ABOUT _____

_____

_____

MY CURRENT THOUGHTS ON MARRIAGE AND RELATIONSHIPS _____

_____

_____

_____

About Your Parent

West Africans believe that a special gift for the mother comes with the birth of each new child.

MY GIFT FROM YOUR PARENT WAS _____

_____

YOUR PARENT WAS BORN ON _____

AT _____

THE DELIVERY WAS_____

_____

AS A BABY, YOUR PARENT WAS _____

_____

YOU REMIND ME OF YOUR PARENT WHEN YOU _____

_____

SOME INTERESTING COMMENTS ABOUT YOUR PARENT'S CHILDHOOD:

PLAYTIME ACTIVITIES_____

_____

HABITS _____

_____

FRIENDS _____

_____

INTERESTS _____

_____

TALENTS _____

_____

[photo]

YOUR PARENT AT AGE _____

WHEN YOUR PARENT WAS GROWING UP, OUR HOUSEHOLD INCLUDED

_____

_____

_____

RELATIVES AND FRIENDS WHO VISITED A LOT WERE _____

_____

_____

FAVORITE ACTIVITIES WE ALL SHARED AS A FAMILY _____

_____

_____

_____

VACATIONS AND TRIPS WE TOOK TOGETHER WERE _____

_____

_____

_____

_____

_____

I'LL NEVER FORGET THE TIME WE _____

_____

_____

_____

_____

_____

_____

MOTHERHOOD

Becoming a mother was like joining a sorority.
My friends and family joyfully welcomed my new addition.

"Oh, what a pretty little brown bundle!"
"Lord, just look at that slice of heaven."
"Girl, you're gonna have to watch this child!"

WHEN I HAD MY FIRST BABY _____

_____

_____

I MADE SURE MY CHILDREN _____

_____

FOR THEIR EDUCATION, I WANTED _____

_____

_____

I TRIED TO TEACH MY CHILDREN _____

_____

_____

WHEN I THINK OF MY CHILDREN, MY MOST PRECIOUS MEMORIES

INCLUDE _____

_____

_____

MOTHERHOOD CHANGED ME BY _____

_____

_____

_____

BABY TREASURES

As I hold my baby tight,
I kiss one cheek to say goodnight.
I kiss one more, so sleep will bring
Sweet dreams upon an angel's wings.

Bedtime rituals always create lasting memories.
This is what sweet dreams are made of.

MY FAVORITE FAIRYTALES _____

_____

_____

NURSERY RHYMES _____

_____

_____

BEDTIME STORIES _____

_____

_____

TALL TALES _____

_____

_____

FABLES _____

_____

_____

SONGS _____

_____

_____

PHOTOGRAPHS, CLIPPINGS, AND MEMENTOS

chapter 5

JUST
BETWEEN
YOU AND ME

Swift needles course cotton, a great quilt to make

One to map past and present, a cherished keepsake.

Like a mantle I wear it

But I'm eager to share it

And before you know it

It'll be your turn to sew it.

Dark fingers stitching, below and above,

Piecing together a lifetime of love.

ABOUT OUR FAMILY

Welcome to our family, Sweetheart. It's our pleasure to love and nurture you. And as the old southern saying goes, "We gonna raise you up good, like beans a'sproutin' and jumpin' in the plate."

THREE THINGS THAT MAKE ME PROUD TO BE A MEMBER OF THIS FAMILY

1. _____
_____
_____

2. _____
_____
_____

3. _____
_____
_____

GOOD QUALITIES IN YOUR MOTHER THAT I HOPE SHE PASSES ALONG TO YOU _____
_____
_____

GOOD QUALITIES IN YOUR FATHER THAT I HOPE HE PASSES ALONG TO YOU _____
_____
_____

THE FAMILY SECRET _____
_____
_____

GRANDMOTHER'S WORDS OF WISDOM

REALLY GOOD ADVICE THAT WAS GIVEN TO ME WAS_____

_____

_____

_____

"IF I'VE SAID IT ONCE, I'VE SAID IT A THOUSAND TIMES" _____

_____

_____

MY HEROES AND HEROINES TODAY ARE _____

_____

_____

WORDS THAT HAVE INSPIRED ME _____

_____

_____

_____

_____

IT HAS TAKEN A LIFETIME TO LEARN THAT _____

_____

_____

THE BEST THING THAT EVER HAPPENED TO ME WAS _____

_____

_____

WHAT I'D LIKE TO DO AGAIN IS _____

_____

_____

ABOUT YOU

*In some parts of Africa, grandmothers
are called Ouma, which means "the important or
outstanding one." I want to be important in your life.*

WHEN I LEARNED YOU WERE ON THE WAY, I FELT _____

_____

_____

_____

I PREPARED FOR YOUR ARRIVAL BY _____

_____

_____

_____

ON THE DAY YOU WERE BORN, _____

_____

_____

I FIRST SAW YOU _____

_____

_____

YOU LOOKED JUST LIKE _____

_____

_____

WHEN I HELD YOU, I FELT _____

_____

_____

MY SPECIAL NAMES FOR YOU ARE _____

_____

WHEN YOU WERE SMALL, SOME OF THE THINGS WE DID TOGETHER

_____
_____
_____
_____

MY FIRST GIFT TO YOU _____

_____
_____
_____
_____

OUR FIRST OUTING TOGETHER _____

_____
_____
_____
_____

THE THINGS I PLAN TO TEACH YOU _____

_____
_____
_____
_____

THE PLACES WE WILL GO _____

_____
_____
_____
_____

ADAGES FROM UNKNOWN SAGES

*Everyone has heard, "The darker the berry
the sweeter the juice." Here are some phrases and sayings that have echoed
through our family for years. I hope some sound a little familiar.*

SAYINGS THAT STAYED WITH ME _____

_____

_____

_____

_____

_____

_____

OTHER SAYINGS I'VE HEARD _____

_____

_____

_____

_____

_____

_____

FAVORITE FAMILY STORIES AND TALL TALES _____

_____

_____

_____

_____

_____

WISHES AND HOPES FOR YOU

YOUR GRANDMA'S WISH LIST FOR YOU

1. _____
_____
_____
_____
_____

2. _____
_____
_____
_____
_____

3. _____
_____
_____
_____
_____

4. _____
_____
_____
_____

_____
_____
_____
_____
_____
_____
_____
_____
_____
_____
_____
_____
_____
_____
_____
_____
_____
_____
_____
_____
_____
_____

PHOTOGRAPHS

A BLESSING FROM
GRANDMOTHER